Seed And

Harvest Time

Leslie Harvey

REJOICE
Essential Publishing

Seed And Harvest Time/Leslie Harvey
ISBN-13: 978-1-952312-25-0

Library of Congress Control Number: 2020911719

Dedication

Thank You, Lord, for loving little 'ol' me so much that You gave me a second chance. I'm forever grateful.

This book is dedicated to my honey, my love, my husband, Irwin Harvey.

To my children: Larisa & Joseph, Irwin Jr (Jay), Darryl, and Lashan. I love you more than words could ever describe.

Gi-Gi loves her grandchildren Camerien, Liana, and Isaiah.

To my Daddy: Lloyd Roberts, I would not have become the woman that I am without you. I love you!

To Wyonna Wardlaw, you have been my guardian angel.

Thank you, Uncle Anthony and Aunt Shirley Hamilton, always being positive and pouring words of wisdom and knowledge into me.

Thank you, Helen Marie Carrie Simmons and Uncle Cle.

To Uncle Ken, thank you for always being there when I needed you.

Thank you, Grandmother Thomas.

Paulette Roberts, My mother, I forgive & love you.

Table Of Contents

Acknowledgments

I thank my Lord and Savior, Jesus Christ, who knew me before I was in my mother's womb. Before I was born, I was sanctified (set apart, made holy). (Jeremiah 1:5) The Scripture states, "I am the Lord, who makes all things, who stretches out the heavens all alone, who spreads abroad the earth by myself." (Isaiah 44:24 NKJV) Jesus is Lord.

Introduction

Are you married and living apart in the same house? Are you together for the sake of the children and for the last name's sake? Do you believe the children benefit from this arrangement or your two-parent home? If this describes your marriage then the answer is no. This story is told through a child's eyes, my eyes, having experienced this firsthand, and almost ruined my life. Even as a child, God placed family members in my life that planted seeds for developing a harvest. Seedtime and harvest are mentioned in Genesis

8:22 (NKJV), which states, "While the earth remains, seedtime and harvest, and cold and heat, and summer and winter, and day and night shall not cease." How can two walk together, unless they agree (Amos 3:3)?

Throughout this book, we will follow the development of a seed through my family's background and we will cover God's plan for marriage. Many people marry for superficial reasons, but there is a purpose why God put a husband together with his wife. First, we will explore godly marriages compared to ungodly ones. Secondly, you will gain a deeper understanding of seeds that are planted into our children as I share my experience. God desires for us to stand on His Word so our marriages can be blessed. Thirdly, we will expound on watering those seeds in a positive and negative way. The devil tried to destroy my self-esteem at an early age, and I overcame. You will too and gain edification as you discover the significance of watering seeds. Fourthly, we will delve into how our actions impact the next generation. Fifthly, we will witness the benefits of raising our children in the ways of the Lord. Lastly, you will see the benefits of the seed that is planted in good soil, flourishing, and producing the fruit of a strong, healthy godly marriage.

CHAPTER 1

Marriage Is A Reflection Of God's Image

Genesis 1:26-27 (NKJV)

26 Then God said, "Let Us make man in Our image, according to Our likeness; let them have dominion over the fish of the sea, over the birds of the air, and over the cattle, over all the earth and over every creeping thing that creeps on the

earth." 27 So God created man in His own image; in the image of God, He created him; male and female.

Adam was alone and God gave him Eve. We are created in God's image. God did not intend for man to live alone. Marriage is holy, designed by God; therefore, husbands are supposed to live with their wives as Jesus Christ has mandated. Apostle Paul wrote in Ephesians 5:25 that He loved the church and gave of Himself for her, as His bride.

At the beginning of their marriage, my parents seemed happy or were they actually settling? Did they really love or lust after each other? I believe they loved each other and were happy. I also believe they were clueless on how to keep the marriage flame from dimming out.

The Bible states in Proverbs 18:22 that he who finds a wife finds a good thing and obtains favor from the Lord. Husbands, your wife is your good thing. There are ways of expressing happiness or joy in your marriage. You are lucky and will be happy as you accept your wife.

When couples meet, begin dating, fall in love, and desire to take their relationship to the next level, which is marriage, there are many things to consider in addition to being in love. Genesis 2:24 (NKJV) states, "Therefore a man shall leave his father and the two shall become one flesh." Becoming one flesh means leaving your father, mother, sister, or brother. No one should be influencing or interfering with your marriage. The momma boys and daddy girls must let go and cleave to their spouse, love them with all their hearts, and no one else (Mark 10:7).

As you grow in the marriage, there will be problems and disagreements that will be worked out through prayer and fasting. Mark 9:29 (NKJV) states, "And he said into them, "This kind can come out by nothing but prayer and fasting." As you fast and pray, you must agree to abstain from being intimate with your spouse. Abstinence from sex is permissible for a period of time if you both agree to it, and if it's for the purpose of prayer and fasting (1 Corinthians 7:5 MSG).

Ephesians 5:33 (NKJV) states, "Nevertheless let each one of you particular so love his own wife as himself and let the wife see that she respects her husband."

Many married couples do not have a clue, insight, or indication of how marriage business works. Many of us marry due to outer appearance, beauty, body, and brains. We believe it is a way of having legal sex, combining incomes, or increasing credit scores. It is good in the eyes of the Lord, one might say. This statement is correct to a certain degree. Then the children come and there are already problems in the marriage. It seems one thing is pilling on top of the other. Now what?

"Father, thank You for the spouse you have blessed me with." Lord, help me to be forgiving and tolerant towards my husband/wife. Teach me to love my spouse unconditionally. Lord, my spouse will fulfill your plan for his/her life. My spouse and I will seek You first before any other thing." In Jesus Name[1]

1. www.preciouscore.com/10-powerful-prayers-for-your-marriage/

CHAPTER 2

Early Season- Planting Seeds

During my childhood, I witnessed how my parents were married, but they were living separate lives. I had one sibling in the home. Although my father loved his daughters and would do anything for us, my mother, on the other hand, was different. My mother often stated that she did not want any children, but she had two. As a result, she was not involved as much in our childhood and my father raised us. The Bible talks about being fruitful and multiplying.

Genesis 1:28 (NKJV) says, "Then God blessed them, Adam and Eve saying to them, "Be fruitful and multiply; fill the earth and subdue it; have dominion over the fish of the sea, over the birds of the air, and over every living thing that moves on the earth."

I wonder if my mother ever learned or read that in the Bible. I often heard her tell my father, "I had them. You raise them."

My daddy was employed full-time as a police officer, owned a mortgage company, and managed a small security company. My mother was employed as an accountant with a government agency.

We were the definition of a middle-class family during those days. My dad provided financially for us by giving us everything we could ever need or want. He loved his daughters to the moon and back. He did the best he could to raise us. My mother did not provide any motherly compassion, love, or care towards us. I can remember many of the disagreements and arguments between my parents. There was some name calling and verbal abuse, mostly from my mother. My dad would just walk away to prevent the arguments from escalating.

These fights went on for many years. I can recall at the age of 10 when my daddy asked me which parent I preferred to go live with if they were to divorce. I replied, "My grandmother." He turned around and left my room. I could tell he was upset and disappointed.

My dad decided to stay in the marriage for the children's sake. If you were looking at the Robert's household from the outside, you would say we were the perfect ideal family. However, on the inside, it was like the shootout at the corral and the saloon in the western days. Since my father worked long hours, we were left mostly in the care of mom, who verbally abused me throughout my childhood years. On a typical school day at our household, we woke up and got ready for school. The majority of the time, my dad would have already left, working late, or just getting home. When he was home, he would make sure we had breakfast, kiss me, take me to the public bus stop, or I would walk depending upon his schedule.

My mother, on the other hand, would only get herself ready and leave. She did not say any positive words. Sometimes she said nothing at all. I resembled and looked so much like my father. Since my skin complexion was dark, my mother took her frustration out on me. I was often called names such as black MF, black this and that, or you are just like your dad. At a very young age, I developed a hatred for my skin color. Every time she would be upset with my dad or not, I was referred to these derogatory names. Those names stood out the most and were the most humiliating words that did the most damage and impacted my life.

According to the Webster dictionary, verbal abuse is defined as harsh and insulting language directed to a person. Verbal abuse is damaging to children, especially if they are at a tender young age. Verbal abuse plants negative seeds, strongholds, and generational curses. I truly believed my parents loved each other. Yet, they lacked Bible principles and knowledge of developing and building the foundation for a successful marriage.

My parent's marriage did not exemplify what is stated in the Bible. There was no honor, love, trust, submission, nor convent. Ephesians 5:22 states, "Wives are to submit to their husbands." Although they attended church regularly, the same behavior continued to persist. They attended church every Sunday morning and evening, Bible study, pastor anniversary, annual choir day, and all other church events. My parents went to church only as an act of obligation or tradition.

Marriage takes an effort, agreement, friendship, devotion, being dedicated to one other regardless of what is happening around you, or your circumstances. Couples must respect each other to be successful on the incredible journey that has been placed before them. These are the factors that will determine true happiness and success. Marriages based on physical appearance only are shallow. As the years go by, looks will fade. During those beginning years, become deeper with your spouse by strengthening the love for each other by reading, praying, and studying the word. Learning how to love and respect your spouse does not just happen. Ecclesiastes 4:12 (NKJV) states, "Though one may be overpowered by another, two can withstand him. And a three-fold cord is not quickly broken." Both spouses must do their part to work through all the issues that arise. Two parties have to come together to achieve the goal, teamwork, always plan, strategizing, and striving for perfection. There is no perfect marriage, but again always work hard by putting forth a great effort. It will pay off and have a great reward. Philippians 3:14 states, "I press toward the mark for the prize of the high calling of God in Christ Jesus."

Planting seeds in the life of a child is setting a strong foundation. Proverbs 22:6 (NKJV) states, "Train up a child in the way he should go, and when he is old, he will not depart from it." Children are like seeds that are planted, (conception/birth) provide water, sunshine (financial, emotional, and physical support), and communication (love: positive words of affirmation and discipline). Once all these elements take root then fruit is produced.

Ephesians 5:33 (NKJV) states, "Nevertheless let each one of you particular so love his own wife as himself and let the wife see that she respects her husband."

PRAYER

Lord, I thank You for every marriage that follows your guidelines such as the husband being the head of the household as You have designed and the wife being submissive. Lord, bless every marriage to live according to Ephesians 5:33, which states, "Nevertheless let each one of you particular so love his own wife as himself and let the wife see that she respects her husband." I asked that the foundation of their house be built on solid ground, not waving in their faith. James 1:6 (EXB) states, "But when you ask God, you must believe [ask with faith] and not doubt. Anyone who doubts is like a wave in the sea, blown up and down [driven and tossed] by the wind. Such doubters are thinking two different things at the same time [double-minded], and they ·cannot decide about anything they do [are unstable in all they do]. They should not think [expect] they will receive anything from the Lord." In Jesus' Name.

CHAPTER 3

Watering Your Seeds

At the beginning of my teenage years, hormonal, or adolescent age, my body was changing. Boys were attracted to me because I was very beautiful. I was often called chocolate drop as a nickname. I had a lot of questions and concerns about things that happen during the teenage developmental years. My mother was more distanced than ever before. If I were to ask a question, she would not answer. She would act like she did not hear me and walk away.

The verbal abuse continued on a greater scale. Since I was longing for my mother's love and affection, my self-esteem shattered. I was confused, angry, hurt, with a horrible attitude, and rebellious. I had very little to no interest in school. Cutting class and smoking weed became the norm. Even though I tried to be promiscuous to feel good, I enjoyed being a tomboy much better. I played basketball, running up and down the bleachers, climbing trees and jumping fences.

My mother and I had many arguments, which escalated to a greater scale. I remember a time when I even stood up to her in her face yelling and screaming. I wasn't going to take the name calling any more. When she tried to hit me, I grabbed her hands, pushed her and shouted, "No More!" She immediately called my dad and told on me. I knew I was in hot water or big trouble because my dad was the disciplinarian person in the house. There was a cartoon show called, "Wait until your father gets home." The introduction verse went as follows: Wait until your father gets, until your father gets, wait until your father gets home. This verse was repeated three times. During the last line of the verse, at the end, three children would say in unison, "We know." They would drop their heads because they knew they were in trouble. My dad would spank or whoop us with leaving marks on our behinds with a belt. He often said, this hurts me more than you. I do this because I love you." As a child, I could not understand why love had to hurt so much. Now, as an adult with children of my own, I understand. I did not know the truth in Proverbs 13:24 that states, "He that spares the rod hates his son, But he who loves him disciplines him promptly." I'm so thankful for all the love provided by my father. More parents should display extra love to their children.

My father was the third oldest of his thirteen siblings and they were close. Eight of the older siblings lived in Los Angeles and the other five lived in Houston. The older siblings were extremely close that they lived within 5-7 minutes driving distance of each other. All the cousins could walk to each other's homes. Therefore, my dad would allow me to spend time with two of my aunts.

One of my aunts, aunt Shirley, was a liberal, free-hearted, free-spirited, and a well-known and respected activist in her community, Los Angeles, CA. She was married with three children at that time, later given birth to a fourth child. Her home was a home. When walking in the door, you could feel the love in the atmosphere. I loved to visit her house. She allowed my cousins to be expressive about thinking, such as what is on their minds, happening in their world, problems, and issues of life. She was very kind and an active listener. She would always pour out positive words of affirmation. Even though she was employed full time, always putting together various community events and attending meetings, she always made time for me when I came over. She would consistently tell me how beautiful I was, which was something I needed to hear at that time in my life. The verbal abuse I endured from my mother was directed at my skin color. My complexion was three to four shades darker than hers. I used to scrub my skin, especially my arms until it bled. I tried to lighten up my complexion. One day aunt Shirley saw my arms. She looked at me with tears in her eyes. She grabbed and hugged me tightly. She shook her head saying, "No! No! No! This must stop to-day." I remember we had a very lengthy conversation about my mother. She was shocked and very upset. It showed on her face. From that day on, aunt Shirley and uncle Anthony (her husband) began to pour affection, appreciation, reinforcement, and favor into my life. They were truly a blessing to me. It took years to undo all the hurtful words (seeds) that were planted. I thank God they were a part of my life. Our Heavenly Father makes no mistakes. It's a part of His plan.

A SEED REPRODUCES AFTER ITS OWN KIND.

Genesis 1:11 (EXB) states, "11 Then God said, "Let the earth produce ·plants [vegetation]—some to make grain for seeds and ·others to make fruits with seeds in them. Every seed will produce more of its own kind of plant [fruit trees on earth bearing fruit according to its own kind/ species that has seed in them]."

PRAYER

I pray for any child suffering from any mental or verbal abuse. I declare and decree Psalm 139:14 (NKJV) which states, "I will praise You, for I am fearfully and wonderfully made; Marvelous are Your works, And that my soul knows very well." Ephesians 2:10 (NKJV) states, "For we are his workmanship created in Christ Jesus unto good works, which God hath before ordained that we should walk in them." I pray for mentors and spirit filled individuals to come to their lives. I cancel the enemy's assignment on their lives in Jesus' Name. Amen.

CHAPTER 4

Seed Produces After Its Own Kind

One day, I learned a little more about my mother's childhood while my grandmother and I were talking. At this time, I had graduated from high school at 18 years old. I began to tell her about some of the names my mother was calling me and the verbal abuse during my childhood.

She was very upset. I told my grandmother that my mother did not cook. I remember her face. My grandmother would spend a lot of time in her lounge chair in front of her floor model television set. While speaking about my mother, "She says she does not cook because she said she did not know how," my grandmother pulled the recliner to an upright position, and stated, "Your mother can cook, and cook well." My grandmother stated that when my youngest uncle was elementary school age, she went to work at her 1st job at the local grade school down the street from her home. My grandmother did not drive, so she walked. My grandmother would walk everywhere she had to go, such as the grocery store or doctor appointments since everything was local in the neighborhood. If she had to walk long distances, then her long time neighbors Mrs. Roopher would take her where she needed to go.

My mother was the oldest of five siblings, three girls, and two boys. The girls were the oldest and the boys were younger. The girls were two to three years apart, then came my oldest uncle when my mother was in the last year of middle school. When my mother was in her sophomore year of high school, my grandmother was pregnant with her last child. My mother became a mother of her siblings. According to my youngest aunt, my mother did all the cooking, cleaning, household chores, and made sure everyone of the children were taken care of before my grandmother got home. Hearing this gave me a better understanding as to the possible reasons that she did not want any children. She had become a mother to her siblings.

My grandfather was employed with two full time jobs: post office and maintenance work for the school district. The house my grandparents lived in was built by my great-grandfather, who I never met because he died before I was born. I was told the story of how he built the house for his family: wood by wood and piece by piece. My great-grandmother and her children lived in the house while he built it. I believe my grandfather was an only child. I never heard him talk about his siblings, although he never said too much at all unless it was about tennis, which he enjoyed during his entertainment time.

My grandfather could have played in the Olympics. I was told many stories about how excellent he was, but due to the racism in the early 1920s, blacks were not allowed to play in professional tennis matches. When I was 18 years old, my grandfather used to take me to the local tennis court to teach me how to play. I thought that I was too cute to play tennis because I would get sweaty and mess up my hair. I can remember him telling me, "It's your hair or your body. Choose one." I enjoyed playing the sport, even though I thought that I was too cute then.

My grandparents were married for fifty plus years. During those years, I remembered they slept in separate twin beds in the same room. This was so odd to me as a child because my parents had a king size bed in their room, and slept together. I believe it was on opposite sides of the bed when my father was home and not working nights. Also, what seemed so odd to me about my grandparent is that I did not see or recall any affection. There was no kissing, hugging, I love you, smiling and laughing with each other. I do not even remember them taking a couple getaway or vacation. As an adult, this was very strange and awkward for a marriage. As children, we watched television programs and saw married couples. Our minds are set on those precepts and notions on how things are supposed to be. However, the examples in my family were very limited. I remember during the holidays coming over to my grandparent's home. My grandmother would cook Thanksgiving & Christmas dinner.

Occasionally we would come over after church because the church we attended was very close to her home. She would prepare dinner and invite us over. I cannot even remember my grandparents having a conversation with each other. I can remember them speaking through the children and grandchildren. They would call the children by name and say, "Tell your father this or tell your grandfather this."

My grandmother was not verbally abusive in front of us, but it was unknown what went on behind closed doors. I can remember my grandmother drinking heavily. She drank vodka straight and smoked many cigarettes during my early childhood. I know she loved all three of her grandchildren, but she was hurting inside. I will never know the story and it's better off not being told. This could possibly explain the reason why my mother's siblings were not close, although they tried to pretend. It showed when we got together for family gatherings. They would walk around the house on eggshells trying not to offend each other. It appeared when my grandmother drank more during these gatherings even though she tried to hide the drinking, it could be smelled on her breath.

My grandmother was not violent, abusive, nor behaved in an unacceptable or unapproachable manner, despite her drinking. I loved my grandmother. She was so real because she just spoke her mind. She said what she felt. I believe this was the reason as to why my mother allowed us limited time with her. I believe my grandmother would have told me some secrets that I did not know about my mother.

During this time in my younger childhood years, my grandmother did not attend church. I don't believe she confessed Jesus Christ as her Lord and savior. When I became a teenager, my grandmother joined the church in the neighborhood, where she walked to church every Sunday morning, and served on the usher board faithfully until she died.

I vented to my grandmother and told her how verbally abusive my mother was to me. I told her even when I talked back and my mother went to hit me. My grandmother was furious. I have never seen her light complexioned face get so red. She didn't ask many questions. She just allowed me to express myself. My grandmother called my mother and left out. The reason I know is because my mother said that I talked to my grandmother and told on her. My mother cursed me out from the top of my head to the soles of my feet. At this point, I did not care. It did not hurt as much because I know I got her back or got revenge.

My mother's family had many secrets and her family were very different from my father's. For instance, I was told later in my older years that my mother and her younger sister were very close but had a falling out. They had very bad arguments that left them distant, bitter, and angry with each other. Still unknown what it was about but I know it could have been resolved. Her youngest sister was very outgoing and always a pleasure to be around when we came over if she showed up at the family gatherings. My mother's middle sister was okay but I believe she was jealous of my mother, but it's just an assumption. The reason I believed this is because of the way she looked at her through the corner of her eyes, cutting them at times. I know now it was the Holy Spirit that gave me the discernment and at that time, I was not even aware of the Holy Spirit. Look at our Heavenly Father at work before I even had knowledge of Him.

Romans 5:8 (ESV)

God showed us love even though we were yet sinners, Christ died for us.

John 1:9-13 (MSG)

The Life-Light was the real thing:
    Every person entering Life
    he brings into Light.
He was in the world,
    the world was there through him,
    and yet the world didn't even notice.
He came to his own people,
    but they didn't want him.

But whoever did want him,
    who believed he was who he claimed
    and would do what he said,
He made to be their true selves,
    their child-of-God selves.
These are the God-begotten,
    not blood-begotten,
    not flesh-begotten,
    not sex-begotten.

John 1:10-13 Living Bible (TLB)

10 But although he made the world, the world didn't recognize him when he came. 11-12 Even in his own land and among his own people, the Jews, he was not accepted. Only a few would welcome and receive him. But to all who received him, he gave the right to become children of God. All they needed to do was to trust him to save them.[a] 13 All those who believe this are re-born!—not a physical rebirth[b] resulting from human passion or plan—but from the will of God.

Children observe many things that take place in the home, but adults believe the children do not know anything. They may not understand it, but believe me, it will be revealed later in their lives. Now the question to be asked is if the children have an open door policy concerning their parent's marriage? Will the parents be honest with their children explaining it on their level? How much can the previous family mistakes be prevented or stopped from happening to the next generation? We must break generational curses, and have Godly families the way God has planned and intended. The Bible talked about the wages of sin and death. Romans 6:23 (MSG) states, "Work hard for sin your whole life and pension is death. But God's gift is real life eternal life, delivered by Jesus, our master."

CHAPTER 5

Seeds Take Root

Seeds take root. Children have a voice and should be seen and heard. They are God's workmanship, hand crafted, and designed by God to do his work in the earth (Ephesians 2:10).

Psalm 139:14 states, "I will praise, You for I am dearly and wonderfully made Marvelous are Your works, and my soul knows very well."

I was an introvert, despondent, disconnected, and maturing. As a young teen, time was passing by. My dad would always say, "Time waits for no one." Between fourteen to sixteen years of age, all of the watering of my seeds (positive affirmations, words of wisdom, encouragement, crying together with my aunt Shirley and the words she had placed inside of me) now were beginning to take root.

Parents be very cautious of the words spoken into and over your children's lives. Colossians 4:6 states, "Be gracious in your speech; seasoned with salt, always be gracious." The goal is to bring out the best in others, not put them down or cut them out.

By this time, I was in love or heavily infatuated with a young man from my neighborhood. He was streetwise due to his upbringing. I was sheltered from that. My dad did not want me to be exposed to that. The funny thing is what he tried to keep from me was what I was most attracted to. The young man lived with his grandmother when we met then we began dating. His life was totally different from mine. At this time, his mother nor father was not in his life. He had very little to no communication with them. He had two brothers.

One was older and the other younger. He also had a younger sister. He had two aunts: Helen and Marilyn. They were very nice as well.

His cousins were all down to earth. They were friendly, open, and transparent. The conversation they had was nothing that we would talk about in my home. They had an open line of communication and were very knowledgeable of street life, which I had very little to no knowledge. I was sheltered from it. Therefore, I was engaging, intrigued, and fascinated by the conversation they held. Opposites attract is a true statement. His grandparents were very nice people. His granddaddy was laid back and quiet. His grandmother was a fireball but still soft-spoken. She was short in stature, but she carried a lot of weight in the home. What she said went with no questions asked. Gracie Lee was her name. She had pistols throughout her home. She kept one under the couch in the den and the other in her bedroom. No one went into her bedroom because they were not allowed.

I loved to come to her house due to the wisdom she gave. We had very interesting conversations.

She had old wise sayings like, "You will not be young all of your life," telling us how to hold your hand while drinking tea with your pinky up, and how to prevent the blood veins in your hands from appearing in your older years." She was quite amusing.

My dad, on the other hand, was not pleased with my boyfriend or his family. My father wanted the best for his daughter. He had high hopes and dreams for my sister and me. During the summer months, my father would take us on camping trips. We were a part of a mobile home club and traveled to many states. We camped out at many KOA parks, along with our neighbors, and my dad's friends. I loved these times. My mother had her friends to socialize with and she wasn't focusing on me. We went fishing, swimming, and had cookouts with the fish we caught. It was our dinner or breakfast. We were able to read our Bibles, meet other children of different nationalities, and hang out until dark. I looked forward to these camping trips. This is where I loved to appreciate the outdoor life and all of the benefits it has to offer: peace, quietness, fresh air, and plenty of greenery. I could be free to roam

and explore nature. We were usually gone anywhere from two to three weeks and most of the
weekends throughout the year.

PRAYER

Heavenly Father, I pray that all parents would
love their children unconditionally. Children are
a gift and blessing to you. They are a reward
(Psalms 127:3). Father, forgive us for not being
obedient to your Word. Bless us not to despise
and break our children's self-esteem. Allow us to
build them up according to Your Word and Your
way. Help us to raise them by bringing them up
as Your desires. Help us to watch the words we
speak and our tongues. We pray Proverbs 15:1-2
that states, "A soft answer turns away wrath, but
a harsh word stirs up anger. The tongue of the
wise uses knowledge." Thank You, Lord.

CHAPTER 6

What You Plant Will Grow

Once the seed is planted, it will grow, but what type of plant will it become? Will it flourish or become weeds? (Mark 4:3) Listen!

Luke 8:5-8 (NKJV)

A sower went out to sow his seed. And some fell by the wayside; and it trampled down, and the birds devoured it. (6) Some fell on rocks and as soon as they sprang up, it withered away because it lacked moisture. (7) Some fell among thorns, sprang up with it and choked it. (8) But others fell on good ground, sprang up and yielded a crop of hundredfold.

Children are people to be heard. Once you say I do, there is only one manual that gives instructions in marriage and how to raise your children from this union: the Holy Bible. We must develop an intimate relationship with the Holy Spirit.

Ephesians 5:1-2 discusses walking in love. "Therefore, be imitators of God as dear children. (2) And walk in love as Christ also has loved us and given Himself for us, an offering and a sacrifice to God for sweet-smelling aroma." God loves us so much. We have to display His love even when we don't feel like it. The non-believers can't see God, but they can see the God in us.

WALKING IN THE LIGHT

Ephesians 5:8-9

8 For you were in darkness, but now you are in the light in the Lord. walk as children of the light (9) for the fruit of the spirits all goodness rightness and truth.

Therefore, we are to let our lights shine.

WALKING IN WISDOM

Ephesians 5:15-16 (NKJV)

See then that you walk circumspectly, not as fools but wise, (16) redeeming the time, because the days are evil.

When I was in college, I worked part-time in retail, and I was still living at home. I had a car that gave me partial freedom and allowed me to get away sometimes. During this time, my boyfriend Dice and I were spending a lot of time together. We would meet up over his aunt's home and hang out. He had no curfew, but I did. I would come home in the early a.m. hours. When my father was home, I would get caught. He would attempt to say something to chastise me. My mother, at this point, did not seem to care at all. Even though I was 18, I was still living underneath his roof.

My cousins would call me and invite me out with the older crowds at various events. I was 18 years old attending twenty-one and over events. Since I looked a lot younger than eighteen, I was given a fake identification card, and it worked. I clubbed every day of the week at all the new spots in LA. I began to live life in the fast lane.

During the spring and summer months on Sundays, I went to Venice beach. There I enjoyed skating, walking on the boardwalk, sunbathing, and swimming. Dice was a part of a lowriding club, and I would go lowriding with him in the afternoon or evenings until the early morning hours. Sundays were one of the best days of the week to hang out on Crenshaw Street in Los Angeles. There were so many car clubs that literally just hung out. We found a place to park and watch the other cars in miles of traffic. There were plenty of people who just walked the Crenshaw strip, which was a popular hangout place. I met all kinds of people, including actors, music artists, music producers, and professional athletes. The thing my dad tried to protect or keep me away from started to become part of my life as I was introduced to this new lifestyle.

At this point in my life, I stayed away from the church scene. I volunteered to work on Sundays and Wednesdays. My excuse for not being able to attend church was that I had to work. Also working was another excuse I had for not being at home as much. The world that I had been exposed, and clueless of became a part of me that I enjoyed. I began smoking weed daily, drank beer for breakfast, then I got stronger drinks later in the afternoon, continuing until I went to sleep. As I reflect, I know it was the hand of God, angels, and the prayer of my grandmother that kept me safe. I can remember being so drunk driving about 5-10 miles an hour on Torrance Blvd. The police were always stopping drivers and pulling over people of color and arresting them. After waking up the next morning, I had no clue how I made it home. I know now it was the hand of our Lord and Savior.

I moved out of my father's home and got my own place that I shared with Dice. The night we moved in, I went into labor and gave birth to our first child. As time passed, Dice lost his job and began hustling to help with the bills. Within months after moving into our apartment, he was arrested and faced ten years in jail. Now I know it was nothing but favor from the Lord because his time was reduced to 18 months in federal prison. After the baby was born, I met his mother, Wynona, for the first time. I called her Nona-bug. She truly became my guardian angel. During Dice's sentence, he asked his mother to take care of my baby and I and she did just that. She went over and above. My parents at this time had moved to Texas, and I chose to stay behind. God and His angels continued to cover and protect me.

Wynona and I became very close. She became the mother I never had, and she told me I was her other daughter. God will send people in your life at the right moment when you do not fully know how they can protect, nurture, and change your life for the good and better. During those 18 months, I grew up fast. Initially, I was living in the apartment that I shared with Dice. After he got arrested, he asked his mother to move Boo (our baby) and I out of the apartment. He did not want us to get in any trouble with the law. I knew he was selling drugs after he lost his job with Aerospace, but I never saw any drugs that he brought into our home. Nona-bug was approved for a low-income apartment, and she gave it to me to live and raise our baby. At the time, I was just laid off from my job and living on unemployment. Since the rent was affordable, I was able to pay it with the unemployment income. I was still searching for work and was unsuccessful. My child was in private school, and the fees were adding up fast. Dice's homeboys (friends) stopped giving me money to assist with the support of our daughter. I applied for government assistance and was approved. At this time, I was exposed to the life of exotic dancing.

I connected with Glo, who worked for Hughes Aircraft. She had gotten laid off as well. She called and asked me if I would work with her to make some money. I agreed because I needed some. Therefore, I went to the strip club with her. I was so nervous my very first time on the floor and it did not go well. The second time I loosened up after a shot of Hennessy and a weed joint. I made over $300.00 in tips, which was enough to catch up on some bills. The strip club was a new world because I got introduced to Bachelor/private parties. Then I stopped stripping at the clubs. I was able to set my own price and receive half the money upfront. Now I was an entrepreneur, making money, balling, or at least I thought. I was still looking for a full-time job during the day and doing the bachelor's parties at night. I continued this routine for one year. After a while, I began to feel dirty and wanted out of the business. I know now it was my Lord and Savior calling me out, but the enemy was telling me, "You need the money."

At one particular party and the last one I ever did, I had a bad uneasy feeling. Glo said, "This will be the last one." I said, "Ok." We entered the room and there were about 20 young guys. We were used to dancing for men 50 and up and fewer men. As we entered the room, I saw the drugs on the table. I still was not feeling good about this party. Glo convinced me to stay. She said, "We will dance and leave. I said, "Ok," as we entered the back room to change into our performance clothes. Approximately ten minutes later, we entered the main room dancing into the crowd. They started grabbing, pulling, and snatching us. We were under attack. If it was not for our bodyguards and few of the other men, our angels, I know we would have been gang-raped. We were pushed into the changing room. While we were trying to get dressed and gather our belongings, the crowd busted in the room. We were able to escape through the window of the second story building running to our car and getting away. That was my last day as an erotic stripper. By the time I got to Nona's house and told her what happened, she told me she had a bad feeling about this party and prayed for us to receive wisdom. Within two days, I received an offer for a full-time job with benefits, which was located 15 minutes from my home. God is an awesome, amazing protector. Even in our mess, He still protects us.

Shortly after Dice was released from jail, we got married against my father's wishes. We were in love and unstoppable. He had my back and I had his. I told him about my past and we were able to move forward. We picked up where he left off and continued to low ride with the riders on

Crenshaw Blvd, Venice beach where all the celebrities and pool parties were. If it was happening or the hot spot, we were there. As the years passed and our family began to grow, it was time to slow down parting, running the streets, and settle down. We needed to start investing in our children by spending time with them and enjoy doing the things they want to do. It was time to move out of our apartment and buy a home. Dice could not see the picture or the things I desired. Therefore, our marriage began declining. We were married in the same house and began to live apart, just like my parents. He continued to party, staying out all night, and sometimes not coming home for days. I knew it was time to end this marriage. It had taken its course. I did not want my children to experience what I had gone through.

After ten years and three children later, our marriage ended in a divorce. The shame I endured, becoming a divorcee with 3 children. I was broken inside. We were supposed to be together forever by beating all of the odds that were against us. I did not know about marriage counseling. I never saw my parents attend sessions. All I knew was that I could not continue with the arguments, cursing, name-calling, and unfaithfulness.

PRAYER

Thank you, God, for being there for me. I am grateful for Your saving grace and mercy. You rain on the just and the unjust. God, I thank You that You are married to the backslider. God, I thank You for restoring me and bringing me back You in Jesus' name, Amen.

CHAPTER 7

Harvest Time

Romans 5:8
God showed us love even though we were yet
sinners, Christ died for us

John 1:9-13 (MSG)
The Life-Light was the real thing:
    Every person entering Life
    he brings into Light.
He was in the world,
    the world was there through him,

and yet the world didn't even notice.
He came to his own people,
   but they didn't want him.
But whoever did want him,
   who believed he was who he claimed
   and would do what he said,
He made to be their true selves,
   their child-of-God selves.
These are the God-begotten,
   not blood-begotten,
   not flesh-begotten,
   not sex-begotten.

John 1:10-13 Living Bible (TLB)

10 But although he made the world, the world didn't recognize him when he came. 11-12 Even in his own land and among his own people, the Jews, he was not accepted. Only a few would welcome and receive him. But to all who received him, he gave the right to become children of God. All they needed to do was to trust him to save them. [a] 13 All those who believe this are reborn!—not a physical rebirth[b] resulting from human passion or plan—but from the will of God.

Matthew 6:24 (NASB)

No one can serve two masters; either you will love one and hate the other, or he will be devoted to one and despise the other. You cannot serve God and wealth.

God sent Jesus to die on the cross for our sins before we were born. Jesus was crucified for our transgressions, wounded, and beaten. I heard this all of my life but never really understood until I began a personal and intimate relationship, seeking my Lord and Savior with every fiber and being in my body. As I write these words, I can feel His presence coming over me. Our God is so real, just like the air we breathe. He is ready for us to come to Him and believe every word, or promise spoken into our lives. He says in His Word, "Come unto me all that are heavy burdened and I will give you rest."

Matthew 11:28-30 (MSB) states, "Are you tired? Worn out? Burned out on religion? Come to me. Get away with me and you'll recover your life. I'll show you how to take a real rest. Walk with me and work with me-watch how I do it. Learn the unforced rhythm of grace. I won't lay anything heavy or I'll-fit on you. Keep company with me and you will learn to live freely and lightly."

The Scriptures above is a great promise of God and all of His promises are true.

1 Corinthians 1:9 (MSG)
God, who got you started in this spiritual adventure, shares with us the life of his son and our Master Jesus. He will never give up on you, Never forget that.

The Cross is the irony of God's wisdom. Praise Our God, for His love that conquers all. Apostle Paul wrote in 1 Corinthians 13:13 (ESV), "So now faith, hope, and love, abides these three; but the greatest of these is love."

1 John 4:7-8 (ESV)
Beloved, let us love one another, for love is from God, and whoever loves has been born of God and knows God. Anyone who does not love does not know God, because God is love.

Once I really experienced and felt the presence of God and His love, it completely changed my life. I know that I was set apart from all others. I knew that I was different and why I did not fit in with the crowd. I knew why I had to suffer verbal abuse. I knew why I was wounded and had deep hurt and resentment towards my mother. I knew why so many things had to happen to me. I knew and understood that I had to help others who were experiencing or encountered the same abuse. God chose me and is using me for His purpose and Glory.

John 15:16 (MSG)

You didn't choose me; remember; I chose you, and put you in the world to bear fruit, fruit that will not spoil. As fruit bearers, whatever you ask the Father in relation to me, he will give.

John 15:16 (CJB)

We are commissioned by God to go and bear fruit. We have a Commanded Assignment to do on this earth we were placed here for a reason and a purpose.

1 Peter 2:9 (NCV)

But you are a chosen people, a royal priest-hood, a holy nation, a people for God's own possession. You are chosen to tell about the wonderful acts of God, who call you out of darkness into his wonderful light.

1 Peter 2:8-9 (MSG)

For the untrusting it's....a stone to trip over, a boulder blocking the way. They trip and fall because they refuse to obey just as predicted. we are God instruments to do his work and speak out for him, to tell others of the night-and-day difference he had made for you. Blessing his wonderful name.

The Bible says we are to trust the Lord with all of our heart and lean not to our understanding. Our understanding will lead us down the wrong path every time. We must trust in the God that we cannot see, but we are led by the Holy Spirit to guide our path. He will never take us down the wrong path.

Romans 8:28 (MSG)

26-28 Meanwhile, the moment we get tired in the waiting, God's Spirit is right alongside helping us along. If we don't know how or what to pray, it doesn't matter. He does our praying in and for us, making prayer out of our wordless sighs, our aching groans. He knows us far better than we know ourselves, knows our pregnant condition, and keeps us present before God. That's why we can be so sure that every detail in our lives of love for God is worked into something good.

Thank You Lord. Praise Our God! Glory to His Name.

CHAPTER 8

History of Seeds, Growth, And Stunted

Before you marry, find out the family's dynamics. How do they function? Are they close? Do the parents really love each other or are they just afraid to be alone? What is the family make up? Who are the important people in their lives? Why are they important? Asking these questions will give you a better insight into if you want to go further in this relationship. I know opposites attract. From my experience, it's interesting and amusing, but the two people in the relationship must have a common goal or focus on improving and developing.

Earlier I discussed my mother's siblings, now it's dad's turn. My father's siblings were totally different from my mother's. It's like night and day. My dad had a total of 13 siblings. Eight lived in Los Angeles, and five resided in Houston. My grandfather made sure all of his children knew each other well. My father would often tell a story of how they came to Los Angeles. Five of the eight siblings, my great-grandmother, and grand-mother left Texas and moved to Los Angeles. The other three siblings were born in Los Angeles. My great-grandmother had saved ten thousand dollars, which was enough to buy a three-bed-room, one bath home on December 31, 1949. My dad said that they did not have much money, but education was planted into all of them. The boys slept three in one bed and the girls had a room. Leaving the south or the county to live in a big city was a different experience for them because they were exposed to more things. My dad was in junior high school when he came to the city. He would often talk about how they had worn their shoes until the sole was gone. They only had one pair of pants to be washed every other day. These siblings had many hand-me-downs and bargain store clothing. His upbringing or childhood was not the best due to a lack of money, but there was plenty of love among his siblings. They were very close and looked out for one another. Even though there were many disagreements and fights, they always managed to make up and moved past all of that. All of them were close in age. Since my dad was raised by my great-grandmother and my grandmother, there was not a male role model in the home.

During my dad's adult years is when my grand-father began to come around and make his presence known. My dad and his father were able to forgive each other and move forward, which took some time. I could remember my oldest aunt telling my father, "Daddy is here in town," and my dad replied, "I do not want to see or talk to him." I was about nine years old when my cousin told me that we had a grandfather that lived in Texas.

Children are nosey and tell everything they hear and see. I never met my great-grandmother or my grandmother. My grandmother died the year I was born. I was born in July and she died in May. The love that my aunts and uncles had for me was shown by displaying the love my grandmother had. I believe she was a mighty compassionate woman full of morals and faith. My older cousins often told me about my grandmother's demeanor. When I look at the many pictures of her, I can see this in her eyes: the love she had for her children. I know she loved all of her children despite their downfalls and errors in life. I know she planted many seeds because, during my childhood, my dad went by every promise that he made to her. Also, my aunts and uncles did the same. Our family had a place of security and a strong foundation of not being uprooted. Education was always the first and of the utmost importance. Being in debt was not an option. They always put money away just in case an emergency arose. My dad displaced all of those things his family instilled in him. The only thing lacking was how to have a godly marriage, which was something he was not taught, nor was it displayed. Love covers a multitude of sins.

1 Peter 4:8 (NASB)

Above all, keep fervent in your love for one another, because love covers a multitude of sins.

Psalm 100:5 (HCSB)

Yahweh is good, and His love is eternal; His faithfulness endures through all generations.

Psalm 100:5 (ISV)

for the LORD is good and his gracious love stands forever. His faithfulness remains from generation to generation. For the LORD is good.

I know my grandmother displayed these qualities and I will carry on this love. I know she loved God with all of her heart. I know she was taken advantage of because she was so kind, forgiving, and had a heart of compassion. I know her faith was strong and she believed in the impossible. I know she loved her children with all of her heart, mind, and soul. These things I know and never met her. I was told I display some of the love and the same qualities that she had. She was a Proverb 31 woman. Even though I wasn't born yet, her traits were revealed to me in the Spirit. My belly leaps in agreement just like Mary and Elizabeth in Luke 1:14 as I write about my grandmother, which is symbolic of being in agreement with the Holy Spirit.

During their childhood, my great grandmother expresses the importance of education. My father often quoted this because it was instilled in him, then he instilled it in us. My aunt, who was the oldest daughter and 2nd of the siblings, was so smart in school. She missed school due to my grandmother needing help with her younger siblings. I was told that her teacher would come to the house and inquire about her absence and speak with my grandmother regarding her education. Seeds were being planted. I don't know what was worked out, but my aunt was able to continue her education and complete high school. Afterward, she became the first college graduate in the family. When you see greatness in others, you go out of your way to help them.

Out of the eight siblings, three of the four oldest were successful in life by obtaining college degrees. One of my aunts went a step further and obtained her master's in education. She taught elementary and junior high for 32 years. She also wrote a curriculum and was great at taking excellent notes. Her heart and soul were into education. She pulled greatness out of others and saw the potential inside of them. We would be in the grocery store or shopping somewhere and a student often approached her that she had taught. They were forever thanking her for her dedication in teaching them. Some even apologized for the way they had misbehaved or behaved during class. I would say to myself, "Wow," and ask her if she remembered those students and what she did. Sometimes she did and didn't remember them. She would say, "Child, do you know how many students I taught?" then laugh. She never talked about her childhood, at least not to me. This aunt taught me how to coupon, bargain shop, cut corners, save, and not pay full price. She would often say there's a better price somewhere else. If there were defects in the clothes, she would show me how to get the item discounted and fix it ourselves: sew a different bottom on, make a few stitches, and create a different design or pattern on a defected clothing item. If there was a bargain to be found, she would find it. She taught me to shop around.

My oldest uncle Ken was cool, laid back, very outspoken, always dressed to impress, and had the finer things of life: fast fancy expensive cars, big or lavish houses, plenty of money, and he was with women who had the means of income. He also liked to gamble, whether at the casino or betting on the horses. You name it. He just allowed you to do whatever you wanted. He was married, I know of at least two times. I know he had plenty of women during his life. He was a college graduate as well but faced a lot of obstacles. He did not come around our house much, or if he did, we did not see him. He only showed up for family events, and maybe at church on occasions. When he was around, he was the life of the household. He was always laughing, bragging, and talking about money. He was a school teacher at the local high school then later he left. I do not know if he was fired, quit, or resigned. I believe he was fired. There was a rumor that he had an affair with a high school student. Only he could validate that allegation. In his later years, he opened a chain of group homes and moved to northern California. He ran these homes, which were very successful. He was wealthy, very generous, and he would just give. I don't know how happy he was, but he appeared to be happy. However, appearances can be deceiving. He was very smart and knew how to get what he wanted by pursuing it with every fiber of his body. The Bible talks about seeking God with all of your heart (Hebrews 11:6 and Psalms 63:1). My uncle did not seem to be seeking God, only the material things of the world. Maybe if he would have or even known how to pursue or seek God, then his life would have been much better.

Deuteronomy 8:18 (NIV) states, "But remember the Lord your God, for it is he who gives you the ability to produce wealth."

Don't put your hope in your wealth.

Proverbs 23:5 (NIV) says, "Cast but a glance at riches, and they are gone, for they will surely sprout wings and fly off to the sky like an eagle."

The third oldest uncle Cleo was the most approachable one of all. You could ask him for anything and if he had it, then it was given. He was a giver and a fixer. He could fix and build anything he put his mind to. He assisted all of his siblings by painting, repairing, or building their homes. He knew about cars as well. He looked to bet on the horses and was often found at the bookie joint, which was a place resembling a small house or very small building. It had one door on the front, but inside there was loud music, dancing, gambling, drinking, and women. It was party central. The bookie joint may or may not close, depending on who was inside and how much money was being spent that day. As a teenager, if I saw my uncle's car there, I would come inside when I was on my way home from school. He would often warn me about coming in. He told me that if I did not see his car, then I better not come inside. The bookie joint was not a place for a child. He then would laugh, hug, and kiss me. He would say, "I didn't win any money, so I don't have anything to give you." When he did win, he would be all smiles. I could tell if he won or not. Many times, I came around just to see him. He would always give kind words of wisdom and advice even if you didn't ask.

He was always filled with so much joy. He did not need or even want material things. It did not take much for him to be content. He only needed a few dollars in his pocket and a place to lay his head. He had his jobs. His prices were the best, so no one could outbid him. His work was quality, so he was always in demand and his services were always wanted. Although he did have much of the material things, he loved his family and would show it at all times. He was always available for us whenever we needed him. He had the kindest heart. He always stated how much he loved me. When I was in places that I should not have been, then he would say, "If your daddy knew he would get you, but I'm not going to tell." As far as I know, he kept those secrets. He was so honest and transparent. He never cuts corners. He just spoke his mind in a kind, gentle, and compassionate way. His words of chastisement were soft, loving, and nourishing, but He would also let me know if I was in the wrong that sometimes I would second guess myself and ask, "Did he just tell me a thing or two?"

Proverbs 27:5-6 (TLB)

5 Open rebuke is better than hidden love! 6 Wounds from a friend are better than kisses from an enemy!

He attended all family events and was always smiling. I remember him most by his smile. Even though I was going through so many issues of life with the verbal abuse in the household, when he showed up with his smiling face, I would always smile. To this day, I miss him dearly, but I know he loved me. He made it known to all of his nieces and nephews. A smile bets a frown any day.

Proverbs 17:22 (GWT)

A joyful heart is good medicine, but depression drains one's strength.

≈

Proverbs 15:13-15 (NLT)

A glad heart makes a happy face; a broken heart crushes the spirit. A wise person is hungry for knowledge, while the fool feeds on trash. For the despondent, every day brings trouble; for the happy heart, life is a continual feast.

Growth stunted of the Seeds

My family states that I resembled my aunt Helen the most. During her teenage years, she was very beautiful. She had a wonderful personality and was very outgoing. They called her a brick house. She was also very strong and did not take any mess or back down from anyone: male or female. When my dad was in high school, he had purchased a mustang that was later stolen from his home during the early a.m. hours. He stated by the time he had rounded up all of his friends in the neighborhood to look for his vehicle that my aunt had already found his car. She had beaten all of the young men involved with the thief. My dad stated that it took him and all of his friends to pull my aunt off of those thieves. She beat them severely. They laughed and talked about this for years. She was fierce when harm or danger came upon one of her family members.

When I was around ten years old, my sister and I stayed the weekend over her house. We arrived that evening and stayed in her bedroom. Before 8 p.m. she brought us something to eat. She told us specifically not to come out of this room and she would bring us everything we needed. Later that night, when I should have been asleep, l was awakened to what seemed like a party. I heard some people talking and laughing then shouting. They were yelling. Me being nosey, slowly opened up the bedroom door and saw my aunt grab a man by the throat and lift him off the ground. She then took a gun and knocked him in the head continuously even while he was on the floor. I was scared and amazed all at the same time. I closed the door and went to bed but did not sleep the entire night. I developed a relationship with this aunt later in my early adult life. She was in and out of jail due to her lifestyle while I was young. She had an expensive and serious drug habit. She was addicted to cocaine, heroin, PCP, and other drugs. She also had charges of robbery, illegal money laundering, and had a rap sheet police record that was quite long. I heard the story while she was in prison. She would beat up the prison guards and lay hands on them severely. She was not easy to contain. She was so strong. They deceived her into signing a paper where she would consent to shock treatments and she would be released early. They lied to her. The treatment was to contain her and keep her under control. It affected her mentally, along with the drugs.

In between her release and reentering prison, she came to our house with a bag of money that was the size of a large pillowcase. Cash was falling out of the bag. She would have on expensive jewelry such as chains and rings. My dad would tell her to leave our house. If she asked for water, then he would give it to her from the water hose outside of the house. I know my dad loved his sister but did not approve of her lifestyle. He despised drugs. He made that perfectly clear. He would often say with firmness, "You can go to jail for anything else and I will bail you out except for drugs. You are on your own." Now I know she was not in her right mind. The enemy or that evil spirit had control of her mind by controlling it with those drugs. When my dad was not at home, she would be outside on our porch. She was always so kind when speaking to me. I would just walk right past her because I was told not to engage her in any conversations.

As I look back, I believe all she wanted was some love and help due to all the pain she encountered during her early childhood years. I was told that she was possibly molested and raped as a teenager, which changed her life drastically. I could only imagine the pain, hurt, disappointments, violation, distrust, disgrace, humiliation, and shame she faced. In those days, counseling was not heard of or absolute. Family members would just push things under the table and wish it would just go away. They thought maybe it would go away. Maybe not.

CHAPTER 9

Seeds Give Life And Need To Be Pruned For New Growth

I learned so much from each of my father's siblings and they played an important role in my life. All of them were and still are very special to me. They were available for me when I called. They did not procrastinate and they gave love and kind words of affirmation. All of them were very different in all of their ways, but each possessed a uniqueness. They were unselfish and canny. As a child, I never knew the impact of all that was poured in me from all of my aunts and uncles. All of them were very protective of their nieces and nephews. My father and his siblings would show up anywhere, sensing we were up to mischief and about to do or be somewhere we shouldn't be. They were anointed with divine instincts and were not even aware of it.

Romans 1:19-20 19 (EXB)

God shows [reveals] his anger [wrath; retribution] because some knowledge of [what can be known about] him has been made clear [plain; evident] to them. Yes, God has shown himself [revealed/disclosed it] to them. 20 For since the creation of the world, God's invisible qualities—his eternal power and all the things that make him God [his divine nature]—have been clearly seen [perceived], understood through what God has made. So people have no excuse.

I learned so much from both sides of my parent's family background, their makeup, and upbringing. I now can understand why my mother was so verbally abusive to me. She had a lot of baggage that was carried into her marriage. She had not healed or was unhealed from the issues of life. She tried to suppress and do it on her own, which was not possible. Later my grandmother began to attend church. I believed she was saved but unsure because attending church does not make your salvation sure.

Ephesian 2:8-9 (EXB)

I mean that [or For; Because] you have been saved by grace through believing [faith]. You did not save yourselves; it was a gift from God. 9 It was not the result of your own efforts [works], so you cannot [no one can] brag about it [boast].

Even though my grandmother served on the usher board and received many awards for being faithful and diligent, according to Ephesians, that does not get you into heaven. The only way is through Jesus.

Romans 10:9-11 (EXB)

9 If you declare [confess] with your mouth, "Jesus is Lord," and if you believe in your heart that God raised Jesus from the dead, you will be saved. 10 [For] We believe with our hearts, and so we are made right with God [are justified; receive righteousness]. And we declare [confess] with our mouths, and so we are saved [leading to salvation]. 11 As the Scripture says, "Anyone who trusts [believes] in him will never be disappointed [or put to shame; Is. 28:16].

My dad experienced some childhood hurt, but it was not taken out on me. He only tried to instill life's principles. Never give up at every no because there is a yes. There is always a chain of command. Everyone has someone over them. Do not stop until you get your answer. The power of education can not be away from you. Research this for yourself. Do not take everyone's word. You can obtain anything you want in life, but you have to work for it. It will not be given to you because you will not appreciate it. If you work for it, you will have more appreciation for it.

Through the eyes of a child, parents you have not begun to know who you are dating when considering marriage. You aren't fully aware of their makeup or that person's background. If they have no family members, then my suggestion would be to pray about it. Ask God and it will be revealed by His Spirit. Discernment is needed and will be given when inquired. When dating, do not get side-tracked with the red flags or warning signs.

Conclusion

Seed has grown, flourished and started bearing fruit.

Marriage is not easy. It requires plenty of work and years of learning and getting to know each other naturally and spiritually as the two of you come together as one just as the Bible states. There is no quick, easy fix. I am on my second marriage and last marriage. My husband is who God sent to me: my Boaz. We are currently on the Marriage Made Alive Ministry (MMA) team at our church Word of Restoration International Church. Being a part of an organization with other married couples has also assisted in bringing new ideas, and structure for us to continue to build. At the beginning of our marriage, we had no clue what marriage consisted of. Although both of us had been married before and had not experience seeing long-lasting marriages, we were clueless. But we decided to trust God and search the Scriptures to find out what the Bible says about marriage. Being associated with other married couples who value, respect, and love their spouse really helps us on this journey.

The first agreement we made was divorce was not an option. We vowed to go through all of the challenges and difficulties together. We have had many ups and downs, ins and outs, but we stick to praying our way through. Communication is a requirement. Many times, we just sit and talk. Even after ten years of marriage, we are still learning and improving daily. We have also agreed to find ways of approaching our differences daily. We have agreed not to argue over money or in front of our children. God is doing a work in us and I give Him Glory.

"Marriage is a gift." It's an amazing blessing from God. Yet often, the greatest gifts in life are not always cherished the way they should. Maybe because life gets busy, or we get hurried and distracted. Maybe because we start to take one another for granted, or we disagree and let resentments hang on longer than they should. Do not give the enemy a window. Learn how to recognize the attack of the enemy and cast him down with the glory of God.

"A healthy Covenant Marriage is one that allows a man and a woman to come together to love, laugh, and live life to the fullest. Having the courage to ask for forgiveness when I am wrong and to accept it when I'm in the right," without the I "I told you so's." (Solomon 8:6-7)

The baggage we bring along from our past doesn't help much either. What worked for us as two individuals, coping with the everyday stresses of life, may not work so well when joined as "one." We spin our wheels comparing our own marriage to the next one over, complaining about the problems, falsely thinking it might propel the other to action. We long for brighter tomorrows, but instead get stuck, in regret and hurt. We begin to drift away. And sadly, many times, we start looking for the nearest door marked or "Exit."

There's a battle over marriages today, and the enemy would love nothing more than to destroy yours, and to bring you down. Don't let him win. You have the victory.

The enemy's aim – to destroy. God's aim – to build up.

In all of the talk about marriage, defending our views, or pointing out differences, we have to ask ourselves one question...have we prayed? I mean, really prayed, consistently, over them. And if not, then who is praying?

God promises in Isaiah 55:11 (ESV) that "His word will not return empty, without accomplishing great things."

There's no magic formula in praying verses and words, but there is power through the Spirit of God. And there's power in His Truth to bring forgiveness, healing, renewal, and restoration - no matter how bad things may seem. His reach is big. His love is huge. His grace covers all.

Prayer + God's Word = Power – the pathway for Him to do miraculous things.

Inside of you, God put seeds of greatness. Those seeds are to germinate and blossom, that is the will of God for your life. Satan has tried to mess the harvest up by getting mankind off into sin. But Jesus came and now you have been born again and those seeds are renewed in you. "If any man be in Christ" (2 Corinthians 5:17) is what the Scripture says translates to mean "You are destined for greatness!"

SCRIPTURES

2 Corinthians 3:17
Now who the Spirit set free is free indeed.

Philippians 4:7 (ESV)
And the peace of God which suppresses all understanding, will guard your hearts and mind through Christ Jesus.

Psalms 37:23 (NKJV)

The steps of a good man or ordered by the Lord, And He'd delights in his way.

≈

1 Corinthians 3: 6-9

I planted the seeds, watered, but God gave the increase.

Isaiah 55:11 (ESV)

His word will not return empty, without ac-complishing great things.

Proverbs 27:5-6 (TLB)

Open rebuke is better than hidden love! Wounds from a friend are better than kisses from an enemy!

Isaiah 44:24 (NKJV)

I am the Lord, who makes all things, who stretches out the heavens all alone, who spreads abroad the earth by myself. Jesus is Lord.

About The Author

Leslie Harvey has committed her life to serve God. In May 2018, Mrs. Harvey was on an airplane and asked God to give her discernment; once the plane landed, Apostle John Eckhardt was speaking on discernment. Later, through divine intervention, she connected with Prophetess Kimberly Mosses, joined the tongues of fire, and enrolled in the school of the prophets. Leslie Harvey is a dedicated active member of Word of

Restoration International Church in Rosharon, Texas, serving in the Marriage Ministry and Royal Priesthood Children's Ministry. She obtained her Bachelor's degree in Business Management from the University of Phoenix and owns Holly Gardens Young Adult home, where she instructs young adults how to become productive in society. She is a certified Christian Counselor who loves to pray, intercede, and assist others.

References:

1. Merriam-Webster. (n.d.). Verbal abuse. In Merriam-Webster.com dictionary. Retrieved March 28, 2020, from https://www.merriam-webster.com/dictionary/verbal%20abuse

2. FEBRUARY 23, 2017, www.preciouscore.com/10-powerful-prayers-for-your-marriage/.

3. McDaniels,;D. (2016). 40 Powerful Blessings to Pray over Your Marriage." Marriage is a gift – an amazing blessing from God". www.crosswalk.com.

4. Betty Barnes, October 18, 2019, A healthy Covenant Marriage is one that allows a man and a woman to come together to love, laugh, and live life to the fullest. Having the courage of ask for forgiveness when I am wrong and to accept it when I'm in the right", without the I told you so's. Solomon 8:6-7 http://www.facebook.com/group.

Index

C

cars, 40, 64

Cash, 68

child, 13, 19, 64

children, 2, 8, 11, 24, 26, 30–31, 35–36, 38–39, 46, 56, 58–59

church, 5, 12, 26–28, 73

closed doors, 26

clueless, 5, 77

conversations, 34, 69

D

daughters, 8–9, 35

disappointments, 69

discernment, 82

dollars, 65

dominion, 4, 9

drugs, 68

E

earth, 4, 9, 20, 52, 81

education, 58, 60, 74

Made in the USA
Middletown, DE
25 August 2020